Best practice in regeneration

Because it works

Tony Trott

The POLICY PRESS

First published in Great Britain in November 2002 by

The Policy Press
34 Tyndall's Park Road
Bristol BS8 1PY
UK

Tel no +44 (0)117 954 6800
Fax no +44 (0)117 973 7308
E-mail tpp-info@bristol.ac.uk
www.policypress.org.uk

Published for the Joseph Rowntree Foundation by The Policy Press

ISBN 1 86134 455 4

Tony Trott is a consultant specialising in effective social interventions.

The **Joseph Rowntree Foundation** has supported this project as part of its programme of research and innovative development projects, which it hopes will be of value to policy makers, practitioners and service users. The facts presented and views expressed in this report are, however, those of the author and not necessarily those of the Foundation.

Front cover: Cover photograph of community art on a Waltham Forest Housing Association Trust estate. Image kindly supplied by www.third-avenue.co.uk
Cover design by Qube Design Associates, Bristol.
Printed in Great Britain by Hobbs the Printers Ltd, Southampton.

Contents

Acknowledgements

I am grateful to the Joseph Rowntree Foundation for funding the project, and for taking a close, supportive, and critical interest in the issues being explored. Particular thanks go to Richard Best for the initial configuration and his ongoing involvement; and to Peter Marcus for his active engagement both in practical matters, and in the development of the key themes which emerged in the course of the project.

This work could not have happened without the interest and involvement of the four regeneration programmes which came together for the project. People throughout these organisations, and their partners, participated in the wide range of activities promoted by the project, and have hence contributed to the lessons which have been learned. Particular thanks go to:

Richard Clark and Philip James at the *Focus Housing Group*

Ken Bartlett, Kamal Faizi, Sue Bickler and Debbie Bednarek at the *Stepney Housing and Development Agency*

Andrea Titterington and Bob Young at *Maritime Housing Association* and the *Tranmere Regeneration Partnership*

Paul McCabe at the *York Regeneration Partnership*.

1

Introduction

The last 10 years have seen increasing recognition that regeneration which concentrates only on bricks and mortar is likely to fail – and in many cases the failure comes long before the bricks and mortar have been paid for. It was not surprising then that the National Strategy Action Plan for neighbourhood renewal, launched by the Social Exclusion Unit in 2001, targets problems in the local economy, social organisation and infrastructure, rather than the physical condition of the social housing stock.

However, with this new approach it is critical that two aspects of conventional capital programmes are brought into the neighbourhood renewal agenda.

First, there are, and will continue to be, major capital interventions which set out to tackle poor quality housing over a relatively short period. How can the capital spend process contribute to the new agenda so as to secure wider and more lasting benefits?

Second, social housing organisations are in it for the duration. Their ongoing, routine, revenue-led business as landlords outlasts the capital interventions. How do they feed into the new agenda?

Although this project predated the Social Exclusion Unit's report, its focus is on the integration of these issues as being central to the success of neighbourhood renewal activities.

The project worked with, and sometimes within, four regeneration programmes, operating in widely different circumstances, and through different means. Nonetheless, they experienced many similar problems. The project had two practical functions. One was to test out four

examples of good practice identified by the Joseph Rowntree Foundation (JRF), both through commissioned research and through the work of its Housing Trust. The other was to provide consultancy support to the four programmes on resolving problem issues which they identified.

This report is not a blueprint for all regeneration programmes. What works in one place may be impossible or irrelevant in another. Although the project started with the promotion of specific techniques, it soon became clear that the process of collaboration between the programmes was as valuable as the technical content. Out of this collaboration, the four diverse programmes consistently found that, despite their differences, they faced similar problems, or problems with common themes. They were able to draw on each other's experience in generating, refining and improving their distinctive local responses.

The project covered a wide range of social interventions. Although their application varied between the programmes, they nonetheless demonstrated a consistent set of key issues which have to be addressed if regeneration work is to continue to have benefits beyond the relatively short time-scale of the specific intervention.

This report is in five chapters:

- Chapter 2 describes how the project was set up, what it set out to do, how it operated, and who took part.
- Chapter 3 describes how the project was carried out, the role of the participants in determining its content, the promotion of information exchanges between the programmes, and the extent to which solutions were identified through the pooling of problems.

- Chapter 4 describes the four examples of good practice which JRF wanted to test in a diverse range of situations, their relevance to each of the projects, the problems in their application, and the issues raised by them.
- Chapter 5 describes the other issues raised by the four programmes, how they attempted to tackle them, and the impact they had.
- Chapter 6 sets out the lessons which have been learned, and the matters which emerged as the key issues for ensuring that interventions will have the capacity to outlast the immediate focus of a regeneration programme.

Scope

Who was involved?

The project arose out of three quite separate requests for support made at around the same time in 1998, to JRF, by organisations involved in regeneration programmes. JRF responded by proposing a linked project of support and review which offered consultancy assistance to the programmes, as well as seeking test bed opportunities for JRF's own menu of successful features of social housing provision. A fourth regeneration programme, in which JRF was already extensively involved, was added to complete the project.

The four programmes participating in the project were:

Stepney Housing and Development Agency (SHADA)

SHADA is the implementation agent for a Single Regeneration Budget (SRB) programme for the regeneration of pre- and post-war housing on parts of two adjoining local authority housing estates in the London Borough of Tower Hamlets. The programme is centred on the demolition and replacement of over 800 properties, and rehabilitation of a further 200. It runs from 1996-2002.

The key features of the programme's working environment were:

- the area is one which for several centuries has been a revolving entry point for immigrant groups;
- the housing is part of a large swathe of social housing, which is the dominant tenure, laid out as estates;
- there are small pockets of old terraced housing street patterns;
- the area is very close to the City of London, and the new London Docklands commercial and residential development;
- these adjoining areas enjoy high earnings which affect all property values, and create an economic and social chasm between the tenants of social housing and all other residents;
- although the estate environment lacks physical focus, residents differentiate strongly between different parts of the area on the basis of estate names and boundaries;
- there is a racial mix, without much racial integration, but also without widespread overt hostility;
- the estate layout, and low sense of community ownership, creates unused patches of open space, giving rise to lowish densities coupled with poor amenity.

Tranmere Housing Regeneration Partnership (THRP)

THRP is a joint commissioning partnership between Wirral Metropolitan Borough Council, The Housing Corporation, Maritime Housing Authority, and Riverside Housing Authority. It operates in an area of older terraced housing, with high levels of low value owner-occupation. It was set up originally as a three-year intervention programme by the housing associations (1998-2001) aimed at preventing decline in housing values, and the consequent risks of abandonment. It expects to be extended for a further three years.

The key features of the programme's working environment were:

- much of this part of Tranmere is old terraced housing and shops, with only pockets of post-war social housing;
- loss of major shipbuilding and related waterside activities means that much of the north of the Wirral is a dormitory for Merseyside;
- the poorer housing in Tranmere is mostly owner-occupied, but has residual values substantially below the costs of outstanding repairs and improvements – typically £20,000-£40,000 worth of works increase values by less than £10,000;
- the poorest housing can be bypassed by most aspiring owner-occupiers, leaving few sale options for existing owners wanting to move;
- recent re-use of the docks for ship repair, and shipbuilding is a slow long-term development needing a completely retrained workforce, which will not necessarily live in the old dock workers' housing of the immediate area;
- city centre renewal depends on drawing in a new employed population – partly through market renting by registered social landlords;
- there are a large number of specialist local interventions which are not always well coordinated.

Breaking the Cycle Partnership (BCP)

BCP is a SRB programme in Aston in Birmingham. It was the first SRB to be approved in which the local authority is not a partner. It runs from 1996-2003. The programme is lead by Focus Housing Group (now Prime Focus), as coordinator for support to a wide range of local projects. The central purpose of the programme is capacity building for residents and groups. The SRB funding does not include any new capital works, but Focus are carrying out major repairs to their stock in the area as part of the programme, from their own resources.

The key features of the programme's working environment were:

- Aston abuts the city centre, but does not benefit from it economically;
- it has high levels of unemployment;
- it is predominantly residential and split geographically into post-war council housing, and old terraced housing;
- the terraced housing is mostly owner-occupied and of low value;

- Focus owns around 1,000 street properties, which is about 20% of the older houses;
- there is a range of local agencies, some of which are very well established, supporting voluntary sector activity, and small-scale local economic renewal.

York Regeneration Partnership (YRP)

YRP was a SRB programme led by the local authority, arising out of the closure of a major local industry, the carriage building works, which had been active in York since the start of the railways. The programme centred on regeneration of the industrial site and the attraction of new industry to it. Part of the site is being used for new social housing developments by three registered social landlords. In parallel there was an employment project dealing with training and placement. There was a community involvement programme for the adjoining five wards. The programme ran from 1996-2001.

The key features of the programme's working environment were:

- the loss of a major local industry which was the spur for SRB funding;
- the inclusion of some social housing, and a community involvement programme were essentially afterthoughts, introduced mainly to meet SRB bidding requirements at the time, not because of existing levels or organisation or demand;
- the industrial site was heavily contaminated, leading to expensive clearance works, and complications in responsibility and control, which affected budgets and time-scale;
- the area selected for the SRB bid is very large, with around 30,000 households;
- the new employment and housing opportunities are concentrated in a relatively small patch at the city centre end of the area, and are irrelevant to most of the residents;
- although most people are not directly affected, the carriage works has strong local cultural resonance;
- the housing in the area covers the full range of tenure, and a wide range of quality and value;
- the concentration of new social housing on one site has led to management problems which would not have arisen had this housing been dispersed across the area;

Table 1: Key features of the four programmes

Aspect	Programme features			
Place	Stepney	Tranmere	Aston	York
Type	SRB	Joint Commission	SRB	SRB
Contact	SHADA	Maritime	Focus	JRF
Time-scale				
1996				
1997				
1998				
1999				
2000				
2001				
2002				
2003				
Partners				
Local authority	London Borough of Tower Hamlets	Wirral Metropolitan Borough Council	[Birmingham County Council]	City of York Council
Central government				
Housing Corporation				
Tenants'/residents' associations		Credit union	Community forum	
Other RSLs	C33 + BG +VPHA	Riverside HA		Home HA
Other			Resource + advice centres	North York Training and Enterprise Council English Partnerships
Properties (no)				
New	830	22		90
Rehab	200+	71	250	
Other		50 owner-occupier		
Money (£m)				
Local authority	£41m including land	£1m to RSLs £1m grants		£2.3m
Central government	£15m SRB		£2m SRB	£3m SRB
Housing corporation	£22m	£1m		£1.3m
Self-funded		£2.4m both RSLs	£2.7m	£2.6m
Other RSLs	£47m			£2m
Other			£1.4m education	£7m developers
			£1.3m voluntary sector	£10m English Partnerships
			£0.7m EU	£0.2m education
Total	£125m	£5.5m	£8.2m	£28.6m
Non-housing action				
Employment				LLiC
Social inclusion				
Economic inclusion				
Environment				
Security				
Education				
Transport				
Other	Community safety Safe play	Community safety Parks	New businesses Voluntary sector growth	New + refurb industry New businesses
JRF menu				
Lifetime homes				
Mixed and flexible tenure				
Local lettings				
Community development				
Governance				
In house				
Informal partners				
Formal partnership				
Separate body				

- community involvement in the programme came after the event, and after all the main programme priorities had already been decided;
- community involvement was facilitated by substantial revenue support from JRF, and by the allocation of a community fund within the SRB funding.

The project was conducted for JRF by a consultant, Tony Trott, who coordinated the interactions, arranged the activities, provided much of the specialist advice, brought in consultants in other fields when appropriate, and collated and developed the emerging views on the key issues and how to respond to them.

Table 1 compares the key features of the four programmes.

How did it operate?

The process and implications for regeneration programmes are explained more fully in Chapter 3. Briefly, the project operated at four principal levels:

- *visits and strategy meetings:* there was a round of morning visits to each of the programmes followed by afternoon discussions of the strategic issues they had to confront;
- *information exchanges:* managerial and service delivery staff met to review their approaches to specific activities based on short presentations from each of the programmes;
- *seminars:* there were joint training sessions in selected subjects, which built on information exchanges, but also used the consultant and outside specialists to widen the knowledge base;
- *consultancy support:* was available to individual programmes within specific subjects to clarify problems, identify appropriate sources of support, and arrange or provide it.

At each level, each programme determined who would be involved, both from within their own organisation, and from their partners. The senior staff attending the visits and strategy meetings would probably have found time for this type of review, in any event. However, the project also provided opportunities, rarely afforded to service

delivery staff, to review their activities with their peers in other programmes.

The subjects of the information exchanges, seminars and consultancy support were determined by the participating programmes.

What did it cover?

JRF exists to help understand how and why society does not work. JRF has a strong interest in physical and social regeneration, not just from the housing point of view, but also in terms of poverty, the economy and social cohesion. Alongside work commissioned from academics and practitioners, it runs its own social housing organisation – the Joseph Rowntree Housing Trust (JRHT), which has 2,200 properties in and around York. These include the Trust's original model village estate of 1,100 properties at New Earswick.

JRHT has consistently sought out and applied features of social housing provision and management, which it believes contribute to the establishment and maintenance of successful communities. JRF wanted, within the project, to test the applicability of some of these features in a range of other circumstances. Not all the programmes lent themselves to applying all the features, and the project was therefore expanded to provide support for, and review of, other interventions.

JRF's menu of success features consisted of:

- *mixed and flexible tenure:* that is, the use of home ownership dotted among rented housing, with the option for shared owners to staircase down as well as up;
- *community lettings:* that is, lettings systems which incorporate applicants' aspirations to live within the area as a whole, not just their current housing needs matched against the facilities inside the front door;
- *lifetime homes:* that is, properties built to a specification which provides for future adaptations to assist with limited mobility, and hence moulds the home to needs of the resident, not the other way round;
- *community development work:* that is, active support for strengthening residents'

opportunities for creating their own successful communities.

The application of these features to the four programmes is described in Chapter 4.

During the course of the project, the participating programmes raised the following additional issues for support or review:

- economic development;
- partnership working;
- the role of housing providers;
- anti-poverty strategies;
- accountability to the community;
- mutual aid.

The way these issues bore on the participating programmes is described in Chapter 5.

3

Process

How the project worked

The hallmark of the project is that it provided the four programmes with the opportunity to re-examine what they were trying to achieve, and how they set about it, in the light of other experiences and information. The features of the process were that it was:

- *self-reflective:* in that each programme questioned its own activities by searching out its similarities with any of the other programmes;
- *critical:* in that each programme was subject to a degree of peer group review both at the overall strategic level, and also in terms of front-line activities;
- *interventionist:* in that programmes were asked to examine the applicability of the JRF menu to their own housing element;
- *supportive:* in that the project provided the consultant and outside specialists to advise on specific problems.

These four aspects of scrutiny and support were delivered in the following ways:

- *Visits and strategy meetings:* each programme in turn provided a half-day tour of their area and presentation about their programme. This was followed by afternoon discussions which reviewed the strategic issues they had to confront, and identified subjects for more detailed examination through one of the other means.
- *Information exchanges:* managerial and service delivery staff from the four programmes met to review their approaches to specific activities based on short presentations from each of the programmes. These exchanges were used for

reviews of community development work, and community lettings. The lettings exchange included contributions from outside bodies currently re-examining their approach to lettings.

- *Seminars:* there were joint training sessions in selected subjects, which used the same approach as the information exchanges, but used the consultant or incorporated outside specialists to widen the knowledge base, and provide a technical critique of the approach taken by the programmes. Outside specialists were used for work on mixed and flexible tenure, and business and economic development.
- *Consultancy support:* individual programmes were provided with access to specialists to help them explore a range of issues and actions, covering anti-poverty strategies, affordable water, safe play provision, community lettings negotiations, developing coordination between health and housing providers, and community accountability.

Why organisations participated

The extent to which the four programmes engaged with the project varied widely. This reflects their different reasons for participating.

Before the project was conceived, SHADA in Stepney had reached agreement with JRF for a project which would both test the latter's menu, and offer additional consultancy support for SHADA. This early agreement set out the blueprint from which the project was assembled. SHADA therefore got almost exactly what they had originally wanted, and were the most active, and demanding, participant.

Maritime Housing Association, as a partner in THRP, approached JRF for action research funding, which would provide some degree of technical support, and at the same time, monitor and review the effectiveness of this joint commissioning partnership. Instead, they were offered a place in this project, where they became active participants, and made some use of the opportunity for specialist support.

Focus Housing Group, the accountable body in the Aston SRB programme, approached JRF for research funding to evaluate, and promote, its re-alignment as a social investment agency – that is, a social landlord which recognises it has to be an active partner in the generation of successful communities, wherever it works. Instead, they were offered a place in this project, specifically related to the Aston SRB. They were active in the information exchanges and seminars, but the non-housing focus of their SRB programme meant that the project had less to offer them.

YRP were brought into the project because JRF and JRHT were already involved in the partnership, both in supporting community development, and as a developer of new social housing. The York programme was the most advanced, and was already looking to its exit strategy during the time-scale of the project. Nonetheless staff from their Acomb Advice Shop became active participants, particularly in relation to community and economic development issues.

Who else they involved

Most of the project business was conducted with the organisations which first made contact with JRF. However, those who participated most fully also drew in their own local partners. Both SHADA and Maritime Housing Authority brought along staff from their partner local authorities and housing associations, to project activities at all levels. Both YRP and Focus involved residents in the project visits to their programmes.

This wider engagement was seen as particularly important by SHADA, because it reinforced their capacity to involve their partners in reviewing both strategic and operational aspects of their programme. Although these reviews were not always successful in practice – for example, their community lettings proposal fell foul of financial

pressures from the costs of Bed & Breakfast accommodation for homeless families – they did establish a basis of common understanding which improved the quality of these relationships.

Diverse subjects and interest at different levels

Much of the content of the project was determined by the participants. They not only identified subjects for scrutiny or support, but they also defined what sort of forum was most appropriate for each. This led to a wide and diverse range of subjects being examined.

It also meant that the project provided opportunities for staff at different levels to engage in the process. Specifically, the visits and strategy meetings were predominantly attended by senior staff and operational managers, whereas the information exchanges were attended by operational managers and service delivery staff. The seminars were attended by managers and technical staff.

The senior staff attending the visits and strategy meetings would probably have found time for this type of review in any event, although probably not with such different partners. However, the project also provided opportunities, rarely afforded to service delivery staff, to review their activities with their peers in other programmes. In the information exchanges, this included having to make short presentations on the purpose and content of their activities, and hence examine their own work more reflectively than would commonly be expected of them.

Lessons

In the world of social housing and regeneration, keeping in touch is not that difficult. The proliferation of national and regional conferences, and subject-based seminars, provide a well-established mechanism for finding out what is going on. In response to the 'Best Value' regime, benchmarking clubs and arrangements like them are becoming increasingly common as a method of reviewing performance among groups of organisations with similar characteristics.

This project was unusual in that the four programmes which participated in it were, on the face of it, quite dissimilar. What it offered them was a much more intense and multi-layered opportunity for scrutiny and support than is available through conferences, seminars and clubs. The following characteristics were critical in determining the benefits of the project:

- *Small scale:* by sticking to only four programmes, there was time for everyone to have their say as an active participant. No one was just a listener, and everyone could reflect on their own work, as well as offering critical commentary on that of the others.
- *Consistent attendance:* the same core people attended at the various levels, and soon established a familiarity with each other's programmes, so that a body of common knowledge could be called up by shorthand. Operational managers in particular tended to get to most sessions, and became increasingly able to provide valuable oblique observations on each other's work.
- *First-hand knowledge:* the visits to each of the programmes not only fleshed out the host's own description, they also often allowed visitors to raise challenging questions about the direction of the host programme.
- *Multi-layered involvement:* the opportunity for staff at all levels both to scrutinise, and be the subject of scrutiny, meant that the lessons of mutual review could go directly into the appropriate part of the organisation, rather than being filtered (with the risk of distortion or dilution) through an internal hierarchy.
- *Long time-scale:* there were problems in pooling between programmes which were not only of different types, but also at different stages in their own time-scales. However, by running the project over a year and a half, the participants were able both to develop the quality of their exchanges, and to anticipate future issues in the light of other participants' experiences.
- *Specialist support:* the availability of specialist support within the project meant that the seminars and information exchanges could be better equipped. This support was also used singularly within programmes, where it cemented the value to them of participation in the project.

What this project shows is that whatever the benefits of sending senior staff to conferences, or participating in computerised benchmarking clubs, when organisations take on testing interventions they can improve the quality and effectiveness of what they are doing by setting up similar collaborative arrangements. The features set out above, particularly those which expose staff at all levels to peer review, will widen perspectives and expand the range of practical ideas.

Interventions: Part 1 – The Joseph Rowntree Foundation menu

Mixed and flexible tenure

What is it?

Mixed and flexible tenure is a two-pronged approach to provision on social housing estates. On the one hand, it provides for tenants, shared owners and outright owners living side by side in similar properties, so that there is no distinction between the different tenures in terms of size, style, location or environment. On the other hand, it provides the opportunity to all residents to increase or decrease their equity interest in their home.

The ability to offer full flexibility is normally constrained by funding regimes which unwisely classify subsidy as being only for rented, shared ownership or low-cost home ownership schemes, without the opportunity to switch the resultant properties between the distinct tenures.

Why does it matter?

The interest in mixed and flexible tenure arose out of the adverse effects of concentrations of poverty on social housing estates. A key purpose is to prevent social housing becoming stigmatised as being exclusively for unemployed, poor, single-parent households, since this stigma impacts on the life chances of all who live there. Tenure diversity promotes economically diverse communities with specific benefits in terms of:

- support for local trade and services;
- employment role models for children;
- retention of economically successful households;
- residents being economically engaged with the success of the area.

For residents it may offer the following direct benefits:

- avoiding unnecessary moves as household prosperity changes – up as well as down;
- access to the asset value of the home;
- reducing the risks of mortgage arrears and repossession;
- stabilising household outgoings, by making mortgage payments which tend to move at or below inflation, rather than rent payments which tend to move above inflation.

For the social landlord it may offer:

- more homes for the same subsidy – the more that residents pay towards equity stakes, the more the subsidy can be stretched;
- surpluses for the landlord – residents tend to staircase up (add to the landlord's funds) when prices are rising, and staircase down (draw on the landlord's funds) when prices are falling or static.

How does it work?

The mixed tenure aspect is achieved by combining an allocation of funds for shared ownership with an allocation for rented housing within the same scheme. It is up to the developing social landlord to resist siren calls for high walls and security gates around the shared ownership. It is precisely the creation of enclaves which creates social division and depresses values. Pepperpotting is fundamental to mixed tenure. Under present funding rules, the shared ownership option can only be offered within stock built for that purpose, unless provided wholly from within the registered social landlord's own resources.

The flexible tenure aspect is achieved by two means. First, by ensuring that the lease documentation provides for staircasing down. Second, by the registered social landlord providing a float for the flexible tenure fund. In practice, receipts from staircasing up in buoyant markets tend to be greater than payments to staircasing down in depressed markets. As a result, the fund can expect to be in surplus over a period of years. JRHT found in the 10-year period to 1996 that proceeds from staircasing up (net of repaid social housing grant and development loans) exceeded the costs of staircasing down by £23,000.

Application within the project

Tranmere and Aston

The programmes in Tranmere and Aston do not involve any new estates. They are both engaged in existing mixed tenure communities, where property values are very low, and there is not much call for shared ownership. Access to ownership is restricted by low incomes and limited credit opportunities, rather than by high house prices. The tenure issues in these programmes were more focused on poverty among owner-occupiers, particularly older owners, leading to deterioration in the stock, and hence in values and perceptions across the area. However, in Tranmere some new shared ownership houses were built, and were very popular.

York

Within the new housing developments of the York programme, JRHT is one of the development partners. As with its other estates, it will be operating mixed and flexible tenure. There is also an element of mixed social ownership, including some self-build housing.

Stepney

In Stepney, the vast bulk of the redevelopment is being provided as rented housing.

The partner registered social landlords have costed shared ownership, and found that with their high values, it is harder to make viable in flats than houses. This is because although flats have relatively lower values, the additional service charge element which they attract makes the monthly payments too expensive. There is further concern in Stepney that, although a small amount has been done, in general, those who could afford shared ownership here are likely to choose outright ownership at lower cost in older housing in the adjoining boroughs to the east.

The Stepney sites include an area set aside for private sector housing – with the possibility of some shared ownership within it. At the time of the project, the developer was insisting on creating an enclave with strict perimeter security.

Implications

Mixed tenure

Mixed tenure is a response to concentrations of poverty on social housing estates. Its promotion raises the following issues:

- Would it be better for social landlords to stop building estates and simply purchase pepperpotted properties (new as well as existing)?
- Private sector developers assume that values will be lowered by pepperpotting, even though their preferred enclaves and stigma perpetuate overall damping of values. Can they be persuaded to engage in integrated developments?
- The social housing grant funding regime identifies rented and shared ownership properties as separate entities, but at the same time promotes moves to owner-occupation for tenants who can afford it. What can be done to achieve an internally consistent funding regime?

Flexible tenure

Flexible tenure is a response to changing household incomes and aspirations, designed both to protect those with falling incomes, and to retain those with rising incomes. Its promotion raises the following issues:

- Within the social housing grant regime flexible tenure can only be contemplated in shared ownership properties. If it is so helpful in underpinning stable communities, how can it be extended to rented housing?

- The success of the JRHT scheme may be a reflection of the relative stability of the local housing market, which has been unaffected by wider swings seen elsewhere in the country over the same period.
- The application in areas of very high values is limited both because they generate high costs, and because eligible households may be able to get very much more for their money in adjoining areas.
- In very low value areas, any form of shared ownership is of limited use, because the bottom rung of the owner-occupied property ladder is so close to the ground.

Community lettings

What is it?

For the purposes of this project the term 'community lettings' has been used to describe any lettings system which sets out to foster a successful community by taking account of applicants' interest in the area as a whole, as well as their interest in, or need for, the particular available property. There may be a role for existing residents in the design or delivery of the system.

Why does it matter?

Lettings systems which match the applicants with greatest need to the size of available accommodation, without taking other factors into account, have resulted in concentrations of low income, benefit-dependent households, with high child to adult ratios, and few employed role models. This is particularly so in new developments, where there is no established community to leaven the impact of newcomers.

There are clear consequences for the households themselves when communities fail. There are also consequences for their landlords, and for the full range of other service providers – social as well as commercial. Unsuccessful communities are not only painful for the residents, they are also expensive. It is not argued that lettings policies are the determinant of success or failure, but depending on their scope, priorities and

methods they can contribute positively, or negatively.

Within the world of social housing there is ongoing debate about the characteristics of successful communities. This has given rise to propositions about communities which are variously balanced, mixed, stable, or diverse. Alongside these characteristics, a parallel range of allocation techniques have been developed to promote the favoured approach. Within the project a more simple proposition has been adopted, namely, that communities are successful when more people want to join than want to leave; and that this is promoted by ensuring a level of interest in the area as a whole, not by securing a particular demographic profile.

The recent interest in choice-based lettings happened after the project. The systems currently being piloted rely on applicants deciding how they themselves want to make the trade-off between urgency and preference, rather than landlords trying to impose it on the basis of immediate property availability and needs assessment. This new and different approach, while shifting the initiative onto the applicant, is nonetheless working towards the same overall objective as the programmes in the project, namely, to create successful communities.

How does it work?

There are two principal ways of ensuring that lettings reflect interest in the area, and within each of them, a wide range of practical variations. Broadly speaking, one way is for the landlord to measure interest as part of the application process; the other way is for the applicants to demonstrate their interest by the choices they make.

With the first way, applicants have to provide information which shows the ways in which the area matters to them. This is likely to cover matters such as:

- *care relationships:* both caring and cared for, and both regular and intermittent care;
- *educational links;*
- *employment links:* particularly for low paid employment, where minimising travel costs makes significant differences to household

incomes, and for key workers in high value areas;

- *voluntary activity and social links.*

This information can be used at any of the four key stages in the lettings process, such as:

- *the gateway:* where all applicants, or a set proportion of them, have to have at least one of these points of interest;
- *the category:* where there is a reserved section of lettings for applicants with these points of interest;
- *the criteria:* where all applicants are scored on these matters as well as on needs;
- *the tie breaker:* where points of interest are used to distinguish between applicants with otherwise equal needs priorities.

This first way of reflecting interest in the area necessarily involves setting up a detailed and robust system, which can be incorporated into a needs-based system.

The second way avoids the need to make assessments of how much interest any applicant has in the area (and possibly weighting between different levels of interest). Instead, it puts the onus on applicants to express their own level of interest. There are two main ways in which this can be done:

- *prioritising locations:* where applicants are required to put a number of small tightly defined locations in priority order, and lettings are made to the applicants with greatest need in their first choice locations;
- *open bidding by applicants:* where applicants apply, as they choose, for vacancies as they arise, and offers are made to the greatest need, or longest waiting, applicant who expresses a direct interest in that property – in other words, properties are selected by applicants, not allocated by the landlord.

Application within the project

Tranmere

Although there are relatively few new houses being built in the Tranmere programme, the existing residents, who are predominantly low-income owner-occupiers, were concerned about the impact of these lettings. A local lettings policy was agreed between the partners,

including The Housing Corporation, for the 70 or so new lettings in the first phase. Its main features are:

- it operates outside the main lettings system;
- it requires local connection through residence, contact or employment. Once these entry criteria are satisfied, allocations are based on need;
- it is advertised through local shops and residents' groups;
- applicants come to a pre-allocation meeting which sets out the tone and standards expected, and gives information about local services. It includes short presentations from the housing associations, residents, and the police;
- applicants who remain interested are required to sign an authorisation for references and checks;
- successful applicants have to attend an induction meeting with the landlord and other residents.

The system is popular with both residents and applicants. It is increasing the desirability of new tenancies, as well as assuaging residents' fears by giving them a role (but not a determining say) in selection. New tenancies last well. There has been only one re-let in two-and-a-half years, in an area which is otherwise increasingly unstable. The system had not yet been monitored for applicants withdrawing in the face of scrutiny, equal opportunities, or help with homelessness.

Aston

The Aston programme was non-capital, and did not involve any new development, and hence no new lettings.

York

JRHT were considering adapting the community lettings system they operate on other estates for their small new development as part of the SRB programme. Under their system, residents are involved in deciding a proportion of the lettings in accordance with agreed criteria. The intention was to keep the resulting household profiles within locally agreed proportions for single-parent households, adult/child ratios, and benefit-dependent households. Details had not been completed while the project was running.

Stepney

SHADA set up a series of seminars, facilitated by the project, with the local authority and external partners. The seminars reviewed the impact of lettings based exclusively on applicants' current housing needs, and alternatives. The local authority system requires applicants to prioritise areas, based on a large number of small locations. Because of the relatively large amount of rebuilding, it is difficult to know how far applicants were expressing an interest in the area, and how much of an interest in specific new properties.

After the objectives of community lettings had been agreed, the scheme was not finalised because of the local authority's pressing need to deal with the costs of rising homelessness. In the event, SHADA's rolling programme of demolition and replacement, combined with a new programme on an adjoining estate, means that most new lettings are being used for decants for people wanting to stay in the area.

Implications

The experience of community lettings within the project raises the following issues:

The North–South divide
- The problems of rationing in areas of high demand, and marketing in areas of low demand may give rise to different methods *but* they are both fundamentally concerned with supporting successful communities.

Negotiating new policies
- It is relatively easy to negotiate community lettings in exceptional circumstances, it is more difficult to make them routine.
- Clarifying the overall purpose of the housing organisation, as supporting successful communities, makes it much easier to develop an organisation-wide approach.
- Local authority support depends on the programmes recognising that they have similar problems and similar objectives.

- The Housing Corporation is likely to accept policies which have been agreed with local authorities.
- Negotiating with other local residents (non-social housing) is unusual, but may be crucial to successful community integration.
- Residents may have an input to policy and process, but not to selection.

Creating new systems
- Successful communities are not necessarily balanced.
- Lettings depend on the context of social housing. Factors such as tenure mix, pepperpotting, scale and the strength of adjoining non-social tenures all affect the overall community and the role of lettings within it.
- Will community lettings simply cream off easy applicants and disadvantage adjoining areas? Or can the aims of improving choice, and raising expectations, be applied across the board?
- Increasing the proportion of economically active residents may be done by mixed tenure rather than by lettings.
- Community lettings identify applicants who have an interest outside their front door – people who do not just want to live in a particular house/flat, but also in a particular street/estate/block. This attachment to place is likely to reflect work links, education links, voluntary activity links, carer links or family and friendship links.
- The lettings process, and particularly the involvement of residents in pre-lettings briefings to make clear the expectations, may be as significant as the lettings criteria in supporting successful communities.

Measuring impacts
- A successful community is a popular one; the simplest measure of success is, do people want to live here?
- Popularity will also show in routinely collected housing management information, particularly data associated with lettings (refusal rates, transfer off requests, voids turnaround times, cost of works prior to relet), and also in more general management information (arrears levels, complaints, vandalism and graffiti costs, rechargeable repairs).
- If we allocate in support of choice, who will live in the properties no one chooses, the

weakest or the worst (however that might be judged)?

Lifetime homes

What is it?

The lifetime homes standards are a set of design criteria which incorporate the features needed to make life easier for visitors with restricted mobility, and make future adaptations easier for residents if their own mobility is impaired.

They are criteria which can be applied to new build schemes at very low additional initial cost – a matter of a few hundred pounds per home. They include features which are available from the start, such as level access, adequate door and hall widths, and accessible switches, sockets and service controls. They also include preparation for future adaptations, such as walls strong enough for handrails or stairlifts, and space and service connections for a ground floor shower.

Why does it matter?

The lifetime homes standards help ensure that the home is flexible, adaptable and equally accessible to households with or without those currently with disabilities. They add comfort, convenience and safety. They meet the changing needs of residents, either throughout one family's lifetime, or through a succession of residents with varying needs. They are ordinary homes for people coping with the ordinary difficulties of life, without having to move home when disability arises.

How does it work?

There are 16 standards covering access, internal arrangements, services and fixtures and fittings, which can be incorporated in the design brief for new work, and adapted for modernisation work. The majority of them are designated as essential or recommended within The Housing Corporation's Scheme Development Standards. Since they were introduced, the Building Regulations have been enhanced in the requirements for mobility access.

Application within the project

In Tranmere and Stepney, new developments are built to Housing Corporation essential standards.

There is no new build in the Aston programme.

In York the JRHT developments are to lifetime homes standards, but the other registered social landlords are building to Housing Corporation essential standards.

Implications

The experience of lifetime homes within the project raises the following issues:

- despite the relatively low initial costs, the full standard will only be specified where the developer has a strong cultural commitment to prioritising the long-term interests of residents;
- the enhanced Building Regulations standard has raised the threshold of normal practice, and probably reduced the profile of this issue;
- there is limited application in practice to existing buildings.

Community development work

What is it?

In the project, this has been taken to mean the direct promotion, and support of, community-based actions and organisations, within the context of regeneration programmes.

Why does it matter?

Housing-based regeneration has historically been concentrated on bricks and mortar – either as wholesale replacement of dilapidated stock, or remodelling existing stock to tackle perceived defects in condition, facilities, appearance or external arrangements. Until very recently, housing regeneration programmes have always been capital-led, and this remains predominantly the case.

Regardless of the need for re-investment in the housing stock, the reasons for community decline are more complex than simply the condition of the bricks and mortar. The process of attrition which deprived communities go through means that reinvestment is likely to be needed across a much wider range of concerns than just the houses. Regeneration programmes which concentrate only on stock condition can be expected to fail. By the same token, programmes which concentrate only on the quality of other services or functions, and ignore the investment needs of the properties, can also be expected to fail.

Unless residents can be offered some element of ownership in relation to the services being provided, the benefits of regeneration will be short-lived. However, their capacity to move into such opportunities for greater participation or ownership cannot be taken for granted. Community development can assist in the processes of mutual support, greater neighbourliness, which enhances the quality of life, and the realisation of opportunities for resident involvement in the management process. The proposition being tested here is that these benefits will only happen when this is identified as a specific, and fundamental, part of the regeneration process.

How does it work?

There are two essential strands. One, that the community development function is separately identified and supported within the regeneration programme. The other, that the programme contains real opportunities for residents to exercise decision-making powers in relation to the programme, or at least some aspects of it.

Application within the project

Tranmere

The Tranmere programme includes extensive non-housing objectives and projects. It employs a community development officer and offers two New Deal placements for assistants. The programme involves residents' training, improving and coordinating local services, working with schools, construction training opportunities, and environmental improvements. The Tranmere programme is a signposting agency to other local services and initiatives. It distributes a newsletter to 2,500 local residents.

Aston

Unlike the other programmes, Aston is centred on capacity building, and has no new capital element. One of the main strands of the programme is the promotion of community governance skills, both through training opportunities, and through support for emerging local organisations. Other strands, such as the development of integrated advice and support services, and the creation of training and employment opportunities, have a direct impact on the capacity of individuals, and hence the potential for community-based actions.

York

The York programme was adopted without significant prior community involvement. A Community Forum was set up as part of the programme, to act as the main consultative body, and to appoint a community representative to the Regeneration Partnership Board. JRF assisted in the early days in developing the Community Forum, and identifying its emerging concerns.

The programme contained a substantial community fund (£350,000) to be administered by the Community Forum. Although the Regeneration Partnership has been focused mainly on job creation, employment and housing, the community fund has provided a powerful incentive for residents to participate. They have been able to develop a clear understanding of local interests and priorities, as well as acquiring substantial skills in setting up and running an accountable system for distributing the fund, and ensuring maximum leverage. The management of the community fund has been the main vehicle for community development.

Stepney

In Stepney, community development workers were brought in only after the programme had been running for three years. They had just started at the time of this project. Their work was developing along three lines. One, general community development. Two, support for initiatives connected with the management of the new housing (this includes schemes such as tool share and garden use, and residents trained to provide a welcome, introductions, and support for new tenants). Three, economic issues such as access to employment opportunities, workspace provision, and employment training and provision.

Implications

The experience of community development within the project raises the following issues:

- the classic community development model – namely, that its purpose is solely to respond to what the community itself defines and proposes – does not keep pace with the dynamic set up by regeneration interventions;
- the range of activities around which community development can coalesce will be constrained by the way the regeneration programme has been formulated;
- the many agencies of regeneration each have their own agenda which impacts on community options;
- the way these agencies operate has an impact on whether their activities advance or hold back community development;
- the capacity of regeneration agencies to advance community development depends on their willingness to prioritise it by engaging with residents to determine what is done;
- regeneration budgets need to include resources which allow for resident-determined priorities to be incorporated – this is not simply about capital spend, it also affects ongoing programme and product management;
- disparate local groups may weld together in response to external threats, which may include the regeneration agency itself! (the ogre model of community development);
- for residents to be involved in formulating regeneration programmes, community development work is needed many years in advance;
- however, this may be less important than residents having direct control over specific budgets and functions within the programme.

Reflections on the menu

This part of the project drew on the experience of JRHT as an owner, manager and developer of social housing, as well as lessons learnt in a much wider arena through work funded by JRF. Most of JRHT's experience is with new estate developments, and the long-term management of whole estates, and the ideas tested here, were of limited application outside of the estate model.

It is clear from the experience in Stepney that even a willing local authority has difficulty prioritising community strength through lettings, when under extreme pressure in tackling homelessness, and managing the excessive costs of bed and breakfast accommodation. The regeneration programme there was able to support community links through extensive decants, rather than by adopting community lettings. This programme has also suffered from the high land costs which substantially reduce the potential for mixed tenure. In this particular situation a programme to improve educational achievement and, through it, access to employment in the well-heeled immediately adjoining locations, may be more effective than the housing programme, which was nonetheless necessary because of the state of the housing stock.

In many ways Stepney had more potential overlap with the JRF menu than any of the other three programmes, because it was centred on a housing estate. The other three programmes all operated in much larger, more diverse areas in which the regeneration programme had only a small impact on local social and economic activity. Neither mixed and flexible tenure, nor lifetime homes, were particularly significant in any of these programmes – although Tranmere were keen to see an equity release model developed for low-income owner-occupiers. However, both community lettings and community development were seen as potent in all programmes – even though the ways they were approached, and the degree of priority they were given, varied widely.

Interventions:
Part 2 – Participants' issues

The contract between JRF and the four participating programmes offered support in responding to issues identified by the participants, in return for testing the original menu. The issues which were raised fell into two groups. First, a set of common issues, which all four programmes wanted to examine, and did so together. Second, a series of singular issues raised by only one of the programmes.

The common issues were:

- economic development
- partnership working
- the role of housing providers.

The singular issues were:

- anti-poverty strategies
- accountability to the community
- mutual aid.

Economic development

The core business of the main participants is housing. However, they recognised that simply providing good quality housing is not enough to secure successful communities. Hence, many non-housing angles have been pursued within the four programmes – sometimes as direct interventions, sometimes by tagging onto other people's initiatives.

Poverty is the gateway to social housing, but it does not follow that social housing is the solution to poverty. In relation to poverty, the following issues emerged:

- How can the programmes work to reduce the export of the limited cash which residents have?
- How can the programmes help residents to become economically active, and what other support do they need?
- How can the programmes help residents gain a foothold in surrounding areas which are economically more active?
- Can housing regeneration programmes be effective in taking on economic development functions? Or are they better left to others?

Not surprisingly, the programmes did not reach definitive answers to any of these questions. However, they did identify some limiting factors as well as some appropriate strategies.

The *limiting factors* included:

- Employment is not the answer to all poverty. Many people will be prevented from turning to work because of age, illness or dependants. Anti-poverty actions, including work on benefit take-up, fuel saving improvements by landlords, and the like, are needed as well.
- The informal economy may be an obstacle to employment where it produces greater immediate net incomes – although this becomes less likely with people who are 40+ (and have an eye to their income in retirement).
- Long-term change will be critically dependent on support and interventions which help youngsters to believe that their lives can be different.
- Local interventions, no matter how carefully planned, may be swept aside by macro-economic events.

The *appropriate strategies* included:

Appearance

- Run-down areas need environmental improvements (including facelifts and cosmetic works) to make them attractive to residents and investors.
- Use the summer to organise events which put colour and fun and a sense of optimism on the streets, and counteract the grey faces.

Employment

- In Aston, proposed new developments which create jobs may be doing so at the expense of existing jobs. The more specialist or skilled the new jobs are, the more likely they are to rely on imported labour, and offer minimal opportunities even to a retrained local workforce.
- In York, none of the ex-employees of the disused carriage works were re-employed when it re-opened. The Cinderella activity within the total programme (the Acomb Advice Shop) has been much more effective in supporting the employment potential of residents.
- The fear or expectation of racism or sexism in the workplace inhibits people from seeking work outside their own area. This can be tackled both by the promotion of local economic opportunity, and by creating direct links with external employers.
- In Stepney, work to improve access to jobs in adjoining areas (particularly Docklands and the City) needs to be coordinated with other groups, because employers want to manage one placement relationship, not several. Training opportunities for residents need to be specifically matched with employers' needs. Employers need to be persuaded to recognise the benefit to their businesses of Stepney ceasing to be a poverty pocket, and support training for employment initiatives by guaranteeing interviews to course participants.
- In Stepney, housing-related projects, such as the Home Demonstrator and Gardening projects, build confidence and skills in participants. Similarly many of the small-scale projects in Aston develop personal skills as a preliminary to access to employment.

Trading

- In Tranmere, an over-supply of shops (old and empty) may have to be dealt with by reducing their numbers, by conversion to other uses. Assessing the retail capacity of the area is essential if community businesses are to succeed when the private and public sectors have failed in the same location.
- Shops in the proposed new retail park in Aston may mean less trade for existing corner shops. Alternatively, new buyers coming into the area may be tempted to also visit existing shops.
- Similarly in Stepney, where SHADA actively supports local traders, there are too many local shops for local needs. Outside shoppers could only be drawn in by securing a new major retail attraction, which would almost certainly undermine the viability of existing shops.

Retention

- The area covered by the Stepney programme has very low incomes, but abuts areas of very high incomes. Land prices, and house prices (as long as they are not on Council estates) are very high. There is little intermediate housing, and local people who prosper are likely to move away from the area. Various housing provision and management strategies attempt to counter this effect, such as, mixed tenure and community lettings.
- In Tranmere, new skilled employment in the revitalised shipyard is likely to go to people from outside the area. Economic benefits will only flow into the area if the programme succeeds in its attempts to reverse the potential decline of local older terraced housing at the bottom of the owner-occupied ladder.

Partnership working

While partnership working was a common issue, the four programmes had very different experiences. The most startling differences are in relation to the local authority, shown in Table 2.

Table 2: Partnership working in relation to the local authority

| Local authority roles | Programme | | | |
	York	Tranmere	Aston	Stepney
Programme initiator				
Programme co-initiator				
Co-funder				
Controller				
Service provider				

In *York* the partnership was formal, with a commitment to joint working, but no separate body set up to implement the programme. The local authority ran the core part of the programme – the land reclamation with English Partnerships, the redevelopment of the industrial works site, and the promotion of new investment opportunities for employers. The peripheral parts of the programme – the new housing development, the advice centre, and the community fund – operated virtually as autonomous satellites.

In *Tranmere* the partnership was a formal contract between the local authority, the two selected housing associations, and The Housing Corporation. Although no separate body was constituted to implement the programme, seconded staff operated under a separate trading banner, from independent local offices, all funded by the housing associations.

In *Aston* the partnership was a formal contract between local organisations. Focus Housing Group was the accountable body, and provided the resources to service the partnership. However, it had no role in directing the contributions of the various, generally much smaller, local projects within the partnership. The local authority had no role.

In *Stepney* the local authority set SHADA up as an independently constituted body to manage this SRB programme. As the programme is mainly concerned with the regeneration of the local authority's own housing stock, it remains a close working partner.

Despite these differences, in relation to partnerships the following common issues emerged:

- *Piggy in the middle:* regeneration programmes face in two directions. On the one hand, they have to deal with superior, external partners who are more powerful and more remote. On the other hand, they deal with weaker local partners. They need to maintain credibility and effectiveness with both groups, by ensuring internal openness and consistency. They need to be able to act as both external champion and internal neighbourhood strategists, without separating themselves from their small local partners.
- *Commercial acumen:* social intervention organisations deal most comfortably with their own kind. Nonetheless, to be effective they are likely to have to engage with commercial partners as well. They need to ensure that they have the skills needed to understand and communicate with commercial partners.
- *Building trust through understanding:* most of the four programmes had to work within the context of a plethora of previous and current interventions. From the outset, work is needed to understand who else is doing, or trying to do, what; and how the new programme can support, rather than undermine, their efforts. Smaller agencies are particularly sensitive to threats to their autonomy or functions. Commonly, much energy, particularly at officer level, is expended on mistrust and territorial defence. Regeneration agencies need to plan for meeting these concerns, and having something to offer existing organisations.

The role of housing providers

All four programmes have a job to do within a limited life, determined by their funding timetable. None of the programmes are seeking to replicate themselves on a permanent basis, and there was general support for programmes having a beginning, a middle and an end. However, in all cases, existing partner organisations, and separate projects created within the programmes will continue, which raised the following issues around the role of housing organisations:

- Social housing providers are there for the duration. Their interest in regeneration is not simply about the immediate programme concerns, and certainly not simply about the condition of their stock. They need to be satisfied that the areas within which they operate have a future.
- Although their core business is the provision and management of housing, they can only expect to survive in areas of economic decline, by engaging in other activities, and with other agencies, to secure a broader basis of financial stability than the mere availability of Housing Benefit.
- The private sector mantra of 'location, location, location' is more about economic critical mass than about style or condition. Social landlords in regeneration programmes need to ensure that the programme embraces the creation and sustenance of economically successful communities.

Anti-poverty strategies

In *Stepney*, SHADA hosted an anti-poverty group with participation from housing partners to review ways in which residents' living costs could be minimised. The design brief for new and rehabilitated housing already included high standards on energy efficiency and insulation. The anti-poverty group initiated the following additional projects:

- affordable water calculations to enable residents to be given stark advice on the costs of different ways of using the supply;
- affordable water negotiations with alternative suppliers;
- the Home Demonstrator project in which residents were trained to give their new neighbours detailed information on the management of their homes, and particularly the control of the heating systems;
- the Gardening project in which residents get access to tools and advice, to help them use their gardens for growing food;
- a review of the security provisions provided by the landlords, and hence reducing the insurance costs to residents.

Accountability to the community

In *Tranmere*, the project originally had only a three-year life – although it is expected to continue. There was concern that the work it had done in securing better coordination of services would fizzle out. Funding was therefore obtained for a programme of working with residents and service providers, to set up a process of regular scrutiny, to introduce direct local accountability.

The Tranmere Accountability Project is the practical manifestation of this concept. It involves building community capacity and increasing local accountability through a partnership of residents and service providers. This will operate through quarterly reviews of the services which residents prioritise. All partners will sign up to a framework agreement specifying their practical commitments.

Mutual aid

The mutual aid concept is that in successful communities residents are alert to each other's needs. In *Stepney*, a mutual aid project was adopted in which residents were invited to adopt a voluntary code of mutual respect, recognition and aid. This was introduced by the originators of the scheme, Lemos and Crane, who provided initial training.

Conclusion

The focus of central government investment in regeneration has shifted in the past 10 years. Although capital works programmes continue, they are no longer simply designed to address physical conditions of local neglect and under investment. Bricks and mortar still matter to central policy makers, but only to the extent that they are attached to, support, or develop the local economy, social organisation and infrastructure.

Social landlords are in for the duration. They cannot afford to stand by while the communities they serve suffer the ravages of economic decline. Their capacity for effective intervention will be affected not only by their ability to draw in resources, but also by the effectiveness of their partnerships with residents, local authorities and other social and commercial suppliers.

Although not all regeneration programmes are capital-led, many still are. Those responsible for developing and implementing capital programmes now have to deal with complex objectives. They have to examine, sift, adapt and apply a range of parallel initiatives which will both enhance and underpin the capital programmes.

Not every initiative works in every regeneration programme. Although some are fundamental, the way they need to be constructed and applied will vary from programme to programme. Programme managers need to be alert to the experience of others, and to ensure that their delivery staff have access to their peers in other programmes.

Regeneration work which is focused in social housing provision cannot expect to be sustaining, unless it addresses the issues of:

- *diversity:* supporting a range of options for residents in property types, tenure and ownership – through pepperpotted mixed tenure and mixed ownership developments;

- *flexibility:* providing routes for residents to retain their place in the community as their lives and opportunities expand and contract – both through options to acquire, expand and contract equity stakes, and through readily adaptable homes which can meet changing physical needs;
- *attachment:* ensuring that new residents come with an interest in the area as a whole, not just in the facilities of a single property – whether through community lettings schemes, or, more recently, choice-based lettings systems;
- *community development:* strengthening and enhancing residents' capacity to assert their own priorities; to develop solutions both as partners and on their own; and, to hold service providers to account;
- *economic development:* working often in partnership with other lead agencies to reduce the export of limited local resources; to assist in expanding economic activity; and, to help residents gain footholds in surrounding areas which are economically more active;
- *partnership working:* recognising first and foremost the central role of residents as participants in defining problems and priorities, developing solutions, and contributing to implementation; and second, recognising the place that social housing providers play alongside other social and commercial agencies in securing coordinated action;
- *learning from others:* engaging at service delivery level, as well as strategic level, with staff in other regeneration programmes to review the effectiveness of detailed interventions and expand the options.

Incorporating these fundamental elements in any regeneration programme will require not only a range of specific projects, but also, and more critically, a way of working which can adapt to emerging ideas, opportunities and constraints.

Also available from The Policy Press
Published in association with the Joseph Rowntree Foundation

Local strategic partnerships
Lessons from New Commitment to Regeneration
Hilary Russell
Paperback
£13.95
ISBN 1 86134 370 1
297 x 210mm
80 pages
November 2001

Achieving community benefits through contracts
Law, policy and practice
Richard MacFarlane and Mark Cook
Wire-o-bound
£13.95
ISBN 1 86134 424 4
297 x 210mm
56 pages
October 2002

Social market or safety net?
British social rented housing in a European context
Mark Stephens, Nicky Burns and Lisa McKay
Paperback
£12.95
ISBN 1 86134 387 6
297 x 210mm
64 pages
February 2002

Regeneration in the 21st century
Policies into practice: An overview of the Joseph Rowntree Foundation Area Regeneration Programme
Michael Carley, Mike Campbell, Ade Kearns, Martin Wood, Raymond Young and John Low
Paperback
£13.95
ISBN 1 86134 308 6
297 x 210mm
76 pages
December 2000

Home zones
A planning and design handbook
Mike Biddulph
Wire-o-bound
£13.95
ISBN 1 86134 371 X
297 x 210mm
80 pages including 90 full colour photographs
December 2001

Neighbourhood regeneration
Resourcing community involvement
Pete Duncan and Sally Thomas
Paperback
£12.95
ISBN 1 86134 227 6
297 x 210mm
52 pages
March 2000

Auditing community participation
An assessment handbook
Danny Burns and Marilyn Taylor
Wire-o-bound
£13.95
ISBN 1 86134 2717 3
297 x 210mm
68 pages
July 2000

For further information about these and other titles published by The Policy Press,
please visit our website at: www.policypress.org.uk
or telephone +44 (0)117 954 6800

To order, please contact:
Marston Book Services
PO Box 269
Abingdon
Oxon OX14 4YN
UK
Tel: +44 (0)1235 465500
Fax: +44 (0)1235 465556
E-mail: direct.orders@marston.co.uk

Social landlords have a key role to play in regeneration – they cannot afford to stand by while the communities in which they work decline. But effective intervention is not just about investment and housing. It also demands better partnerships with residents and other social suppliers to develop the local economy, social organisation and infrastructure.

This report charts a supportive project that linked four diverse regeneration programmes in different parts of the UK. By working closely together at all levels, the groups involved in the project improved their strategic understanding and operational approaches. The report highlights the key practical themes of successful regeneration – what works and where – and effective ways of learning from the experiences of others.

Best practice in regeneration presents practical options for achieving:
- diverse and flexible patterns of housing ownership, standards and tenure to retain stable communities;
- residents who are committed to the area as a whole, not just to their own home;
- community and economic development to build and sustain local capacity;
- partnership working between and within organisations.

This report is aimed at decision makers in regeneration partnerships, particularly social housing providers. It demonstrates the potential gains when managers and service delivery staff engage in peer review groups with those in other programmes, and shows how to make this happen. It will also be of interest to strategic planners and regeneration budget holders.

Tony Trott is a consultant specialising in effective social interventions. He has worked in social housing for 30 years. Recent projects include: strategic regeneration; investment in communities; new approaches to lettings; analysis of drugs, crime and housing problems in urban renewal; and managing housing associations.

The POLICY PRESS

JR JOSEPH ROWNTREE FOUNDATION

ISBN 1-86134-455-4

9 781861 344557 >

Photograph kindly supplied by www.third-avenue.co.uk

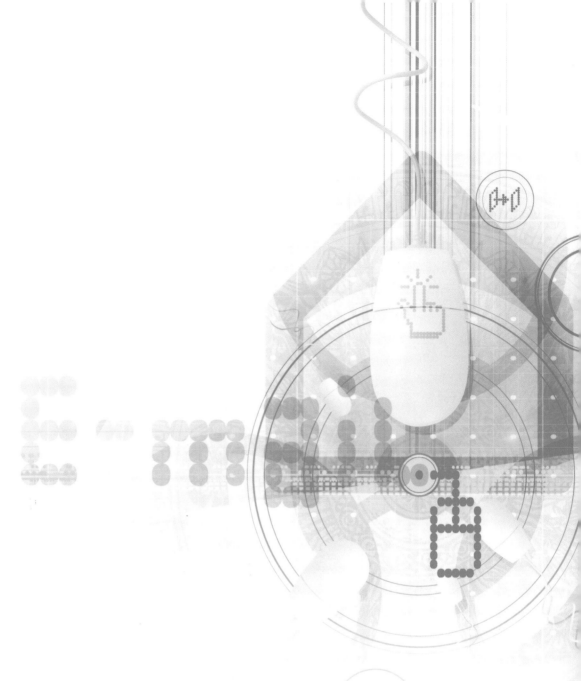

Remote control

Housing associations and e-governance

Martyn Pearl and Martina Scanlon